Cool-Doo Math

[GRADE 3 AND 4]

Bound Volume

(Vol.01 - Vol.04)

www.cool-doo.com

01

Word Problems by Peter Feng
Comic Stories by Andrew Feng
Comic Sketches by Andrew Feng
Digital Ink by Peter Feng

Number
rules the universe.

- Pythagoras (569-500BC)

Jack

Cool-Doo

Sleepy-Doo

To know the adventure of Jack and his gang,
please read *TUM* - The Unmoved Mover.
www.t-u-m.net

Dr. Green

Dr. Z

Jr. Z

To know the adventure of Jack and his gang,
please read *TUM* - The Unmoved Mover.
www.t-u-m.net

Contents

A 20-Minute Call....................................9

A Paintball Game in a Crazy Lab....................15

Rise & Shine....................................21

A Stinky Accident....................................27

Who Will Win the Marathon?....................33

The Candy Catch....................................39

4 Pillows in a Picture....................................45

Laser Darting....................................51

Balancing....................................57

Luggage Lock Combinations....................63

Jr. Z's New Invention.......................................69

The Math Competition......................................75

Waiting for Chips...81

Good Chips, Bad Chips.....................................87

Sailing Around the World..................................93

The Mole Patrol...99

TUM Car Racing..105

Bicycles and Tricycles.....................................111

Cuts in a Cake..117

Who Will Eat the Pizza?...................................123

About the Author...129

Another Fun Book by Andrew & Peter...........131

A 20-Minute Call

Cool-Doo was in a phone booth talking to Jack and Sleepy-Doo ...

Blah Blah Blah...

A. 1 Toonie + 2 Loonies + 2 Quarters
B. 30 Dimes + 2 Nickels + 2 Loonies
C. 4 Loonies + 1 Toonie - 2 Quarters
D. 3 Toonies - 4 Quarters

z z z Z Z Z Z Z

Snore
Snore...

? ? ?

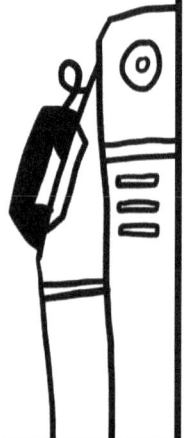

Z Z Z z

ANSWER

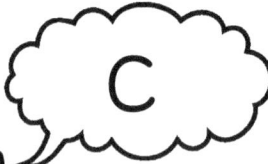

C

SOLUTION

The cost of the first 6 minutes is:
$0.45 × 6 = $2.70
Extra minutes after the first 6 minutes is:
20 - 6 = 14 minutes
The cost of the extra minutes is:
$0.20 × 14 = $2.80
Total cost of a 20-minute call is:
$2.70 + $2.80 = $5.50

A = $2 + 2 × $1 + 2 × $0.25 = $4.5 (✗)
B = 30 × $0.1 + 2 × $0.05 + 2 × $1 = $5.1 (✗)
C = 4 × $1 + 1 × $2 - 2 × $.25 = $5.5 (✓)
D = 3 × $2 - 4 × $0.25 = $5 (✗)

The correct answer is "C".

A Paintball Game in a Crazy Lab

Jack and Jr. Z
were having
a **paintball** game
in Jr. Z's
crazy lab.

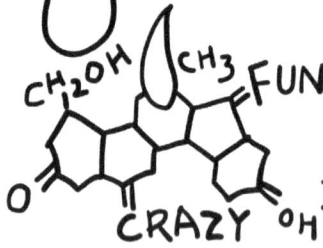

They played 3 games.

In the **1st** and **2nd** games,

Jack hit Jr. ∠ **15** times.

In the **2nd** and **3rd** games,
Jack hit Jr. ∠ the same times
and
altogehter

there were **18** times.

How many times did Jack **hit** Jr. Z in the **1st** game?

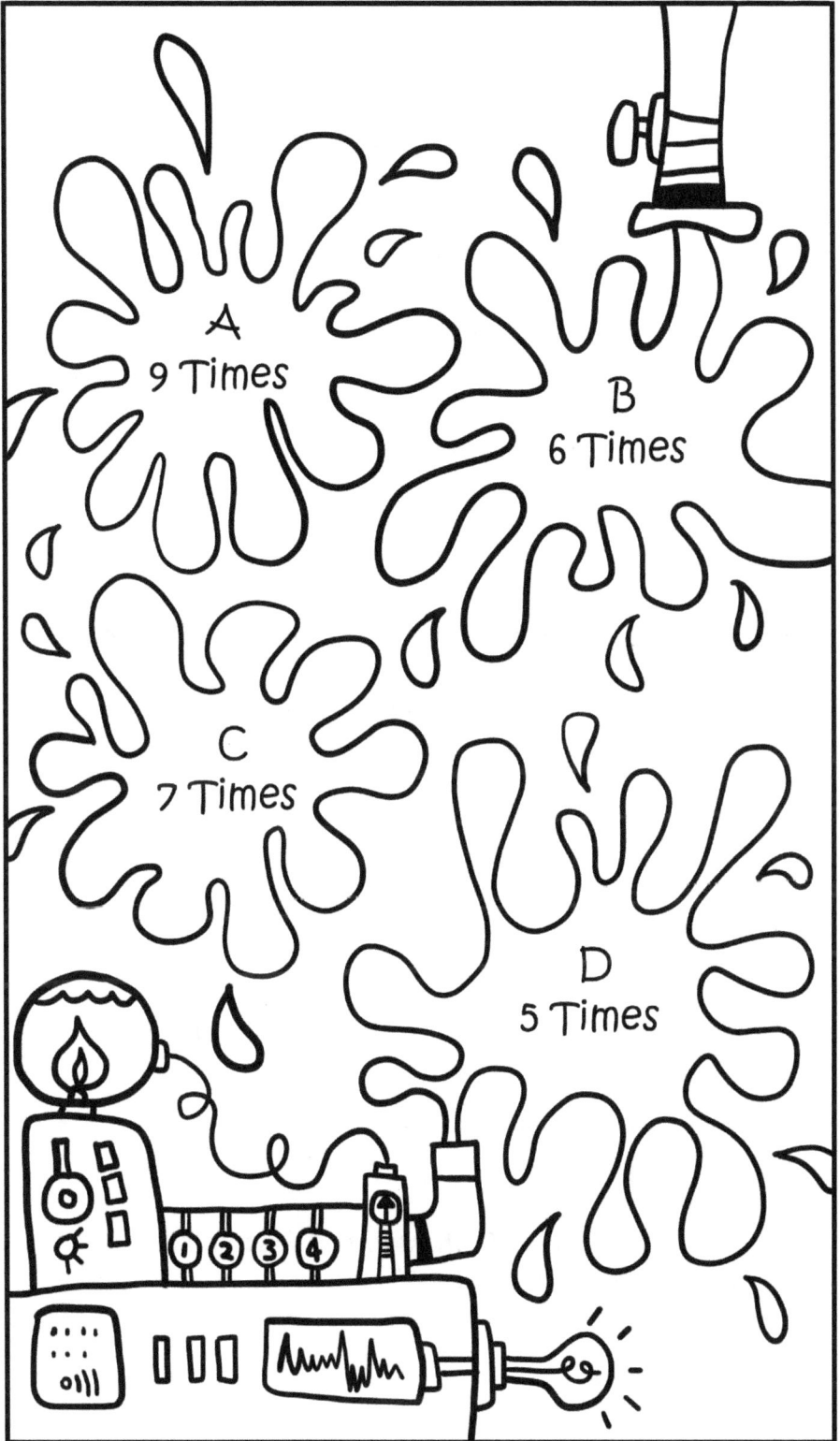

A
9 Times

B
6 Times

C
7 Times

D
5 Times

ANSWER

SOLUTION

Use G1 to represent times that Jack hits Jr. Z in the first game;
Use G2 to represent times that Jack hits Jr. Z in the second game;
Use G3 to represent times that Jack hits Jr. Z in the third game.

Three equations can be concluded based on the story:

1. G1 + G2 = 15
2. G2 + G3 = 18
3. G2 = G3

As G2=G3, use G2 to replace G3 in equation 2:
G2 + G2 = 18 ➜ G2 = 9

Then bring 9 into equation 1:
G1 + 9 = 15 ➜ G1 = 15 - 9 = 6

So, Jack hit Jr. Z 6 times in the first game.
The correct answer is "B".

Rise and Shine

The clock in Sleepy-Doo's room was **35** minutes behind. Now it was showing 6:55.

6:55

WAKE UP!

?!!!

It's still early...

SCHOOL

The clock in Jack's room was **15** minutes ahead.

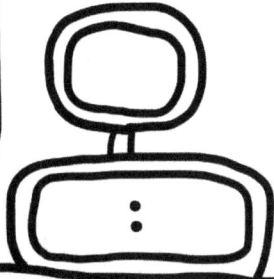

ANSWER

SOLUTION

Sleepy-doo's clock is 35 minutes behind, so the correct time is:
6:55 + 0:35 = 7:30

Jack's clock is 15 minutes ahead, so the time of Jack's clock is:
7:30 + 0:15 = 7:45

The correct answer is "D".

A Stinky Accident

There were **15** weird test tubes. **6** of them had 2 mouths and the rest had 3 mouths. Dr. Z used corks to plug each mouth.

Before Dr. Z executed his plan, Jr. Z wanted to use corks as bullets in his toy gun. He found out that the corks from those tubes were the exact number of bullets he needed. So he pulled out all of the corks...

...then you know what will happen.

But the question is, how many bullets did Jr. Z need for his toy gun?

POP!

Mmmf... phh... phe...

Ha Ha!

ANSWER

SOLUTION

As 6 of the tubes have 2 mouths, so the number of the corks of these 2-mouth tubes are:

6 × 2 = 12

The number of 3-mouth tubes are:

15 - 6 = 9

So the number of the corks of these 3-mouth tubes are:

9 × 3 = 27

Total number of corks are:

12 + 27 = 39

Jr. Z needed 39 bullets for his toy gun.
The correct answer is B.

Who Will Win the Marathon?

Cool-Doo and Sleepy-Doo were running a **marathon** on the beach.
Just one more **nap**...
I'm ready!

Cool-Doo could run
the marathon in **2 hours**
and **2 minutes**,
BUT...
My turn
to take
a **nap**!
Cool-Doo
took a nap
for **2 hours**
and
3 minutes.
Z z z

ANSWER

SOLUTION

If Cool-Doo can run the marathon
in 2 hours and 2 minutes, then
Sleepy-Doo can run it in 4 hours
and 4 minutes. But, Cool-Doo takes
a nap for 2 hours and 3 minutes,
so he uses 4 hours and 5 minutes
in total.

Sleepy-Doo won the marathon
by 1 minute early.

The correct answer is B.

The Candy Catch

Cool-Doo, Jack and Sleepy-Doo were playing a **Candy** catching game.

9032

Hey! I need to get some **Candies!**

Mine!

There were
9032 candies
altogether.

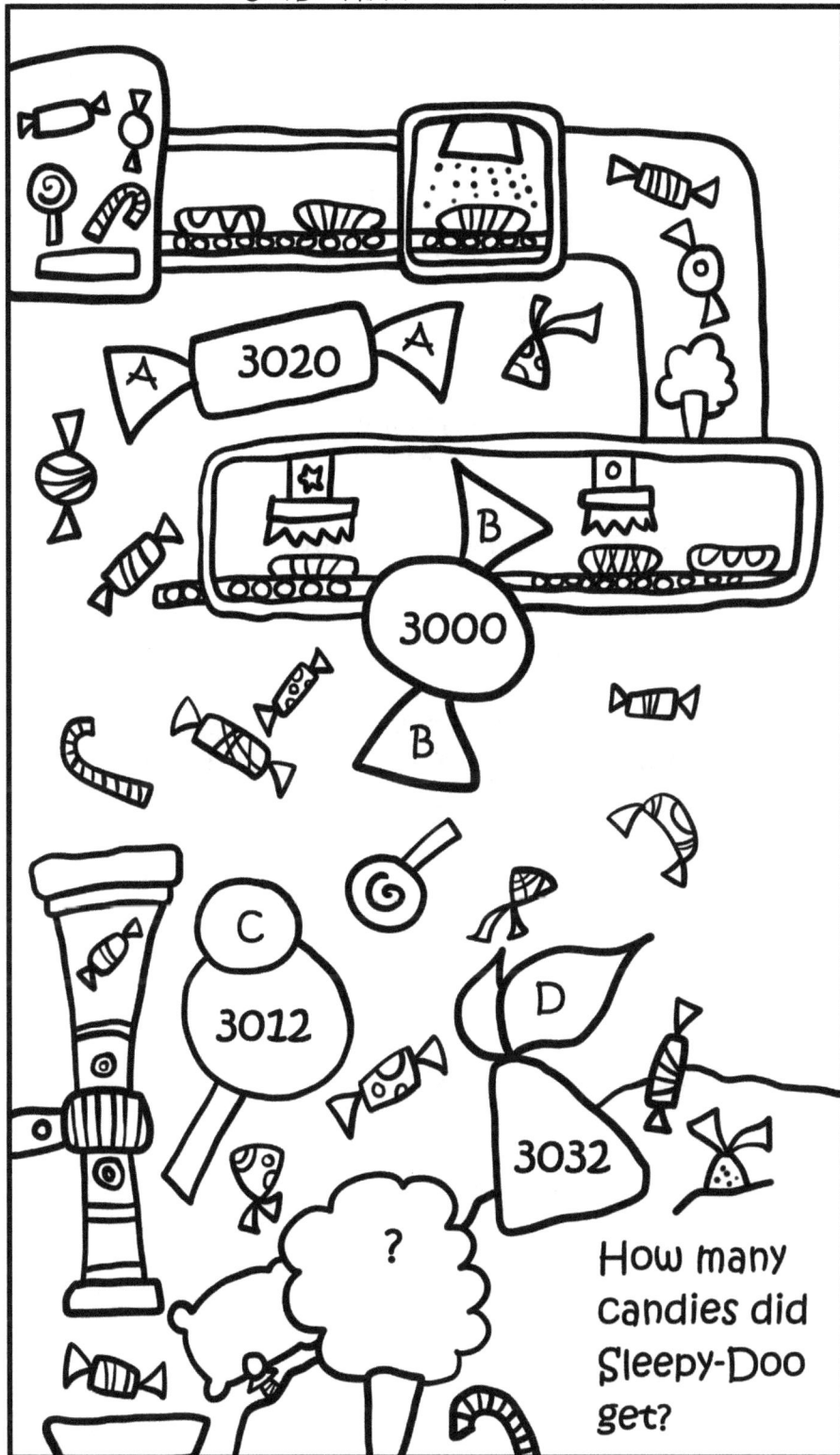

A — 3020 — A

B 3000 B

C 3012

D 3032

?

How many candies did Sleepy-Doo get?

ANSWER

SOLUTION

The total extra candies that Jack and Cool-Doo have:

12 + 20 = 32

After subtracting the extra candies, the three boys will have the same amount, and the total amount is:

9032 - 32 = 9000

Sleepy-Doo has 1/3:

9000 / 3 = 3000

The correct answer is B.

4 Pillows in a Picture

How many ways
can Sleepy-Doo
arrange
his

pillows?

(A) 5

(B) 3

(C) 4

(D) 6

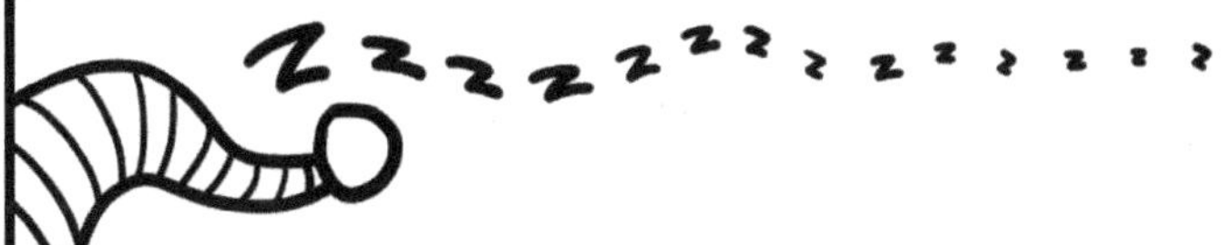

ANSWER

SOLUTION

The yellow pillow can be placed only on the left or right, and the other pillows are in the middle. The red pillow has to be next to the white pillow, and the blue pillow should be beside the red pillow. In that case, here are the arrangements Sleepy-Doo can make:

BRWY

YBRW

WRBY

YWRB

The answer is C.

Laser Darting

(5) Cool-Doo was playing **laser darting.** (10) (3)

Wait!

Can I try?

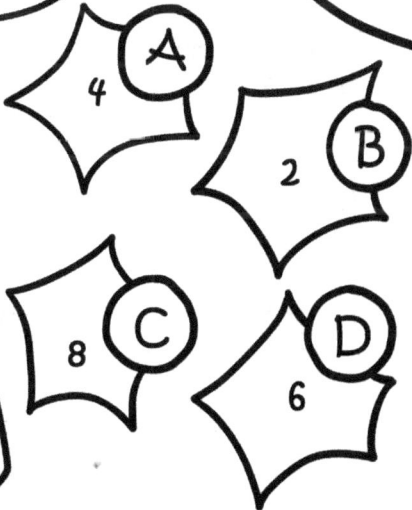

ANSWER

B

SOLUTION

Cool-Doo hits the target only for 5 times to make 26. Let's see how to make 20 by hitting the target less than 5 times.

If he hits the target 4 times to make 20, he has to hit "5" 4 times. He has only 1 chance to make a "6" so that his total score can be 20+6=26.

That is impossible becasue there is no target with a "6" score.

Then, we try if Cool-Doo hits the target 3 times to make 20. To do so, he has to hit "5" twice and "10" once.

Now there are 2 chances left for Cool-Doo to make 6.

Bingo! It's so obvious that Cool-Doo hits "3" twice to make 6.

The correct answer is B.

Balancing

$E = mc^2$

Dr. Green and Jack were doing a balancing experiment.

Jack, I have a question for **you!**

The weight of **1** big ball and **8** small balls were equal to the weight of **2** big balls.

Again!

How many grams does 1 big ball weigh?
Jack?!
!?#
A
85g
40g
B
30g
C
D
45g
ZZzzzz
Not that!

ANSWER

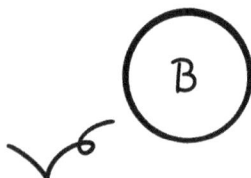

B

SOLUTION

Eight small balls weigh:

5g × 8 = 40g

Then, 1 big ball + 40g = 2 big balls.

So, 1 big ball = 40g

The answer is B.

Luggage Lock

COMBINATIONS

Jack's luggage lock combination was 3-3-3-3.

Jack, Cool-Doo and Sleepy-Doo were in the Space Camp. Their luggage lock combinations followed the same rule.

This is **Mine!**

What was Sleepy-Doo's last digit of his luggage lock combination?

A. 62

B. 60

C. 59

D. 45

Wow! It's a **paradise** of pillows!

Wake up! These are suitcases!

Oh, Well...

ANSWER

SOLUTION

Let's check Cool-Doo's combination first:
4 × 2 - 3 = 5, 5 × 2 - 3 = 7, 7 × 2 - 3 = 11

Then, the pattern looks like:
n × 2 - 3 = the next digit

Let's double-check if this pattern applies for Jack's combination:
3 × 2 - 3 = 3, 3 × 2 - 3 = 3, 3 × 2 - 3 = 3

Hooray! It's correct!

Now we can get Sleepy-Doo's combination:

10 × 2 - 3 = 17, 17 × 2 - 3 = 31, 31 × 2 - 3 = 59

The correct answer is C.

Jr. Z's New Invention

On Z Island, it took the patrol pod **30** minutes to drive around the island.

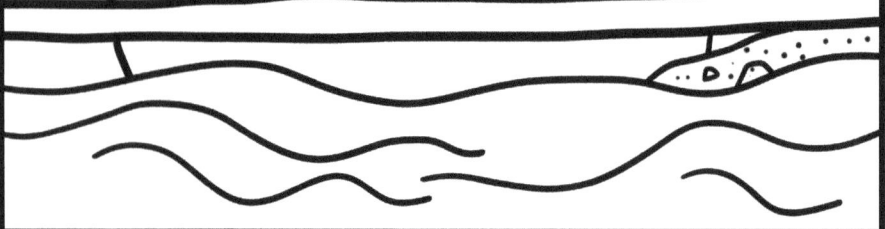

I made a flying drone.
It took **20** minutes
to fly around the island.

If the patrol pod and the flying drone departed together at **8:00pm**, when was the earliest time they would meet again?

I think I left my tacos in the oven!

ANSWER

A

SOLUTION

This is a LCM (Lowest Common Multiples) question.

Find the LCM for 20 and 30.
The prime factors for 20 are: 2×2×5
The prime factors for 30 are: 2×3×5
The LCM for 20 and 30 is: 2×2×3×5=60

Since 60 is the smallest number that both 20 and 30 can be divided into equally, the pod and the drone will meet again 60 minutes after 8:00 pm.
It should be 9:00pm.

The correct answer is A.

The MATH COMPETITION

They needed to get an average of 85 to be eligible. Unfortunately, Jack's score was 83, and Cool-Doo's score was 84.

Darn it! So close!

Come on, guys!

I'm gonna go buy some more chips!

84

CHIPS

83

Uh oh!

To make the team eligible, what was the minimum score for Sleepy-Doo to pass his test?

Maybe next time...

My Turn!

Maybe...

84

CHIPS

83

ANSWER

(D)

SOLUTION

Jack needs to score 2 more points to get 85.

Cool-Doo needs to score 1 more point to get 85.

Sleepy-Doo needs to score at least 3 more points to make up for Jack and Cool-Doo, so he has to get at least 85+3=88.

The correct answer is D.

? : ?

Waiting for CHiPs

TUM classic

When the delivery guy called to tell when the *TUM CHIPS* would arrive, Sleepy-Doo received the call.

Ha ha! I'm gonna eat the crumbs!

The *TUM CHIPS* will arrive at the time when what is left of the day is **one third** of the time that has passed. Remember that our clock is a **24-hour** digital clock!

Jack was puzzled. Could you help him figure out what time his *TUM CHIPS* would arrive?

ANSWER

SOLUTION

If there are 3 units for the time that has passed, there will be 1 unit for the time that is left of the day. Altogether there are 4 units for the whole day. Each unit is 24/4=6hrs. 3 units is 6×3=18hrs.

So the chips will arrive at 18:00.

There is another way to solve the problem:

If we use X to represent the arriving time, we can have $24 - X = X / 3 \rightarrow 72 - 3X = X$ $\rightarrow 72 = 4X \rightarrow X = 18$.

So the chips will arrive at 18:00.

The correct answer is B.

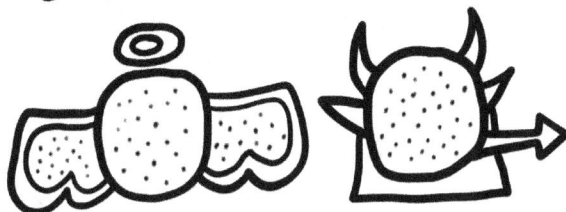

GOOD CHIPS
BAD CHIPS

I'm making **17** bags of "special "*TUM CHIPS*. To surprise Jack, I'm gonna put my super fire sauce chips in these bags and mix them up with Jack's real *TUM CHIPS*.

Hee, hee, hee!

Oh yeah!

Can I have some?

When Jack counted his potato chip bags, he found out that there were **80** bags in total with **2** kinds of chips. One was *TUM CHIPS* and the other was *YUMMY YUMMY CHIPS*.

There were **24** bags of *YUMMY YUMMY CHIPS*.

Maybe the next bag...

Mmm! TUM yummy!

AHHH! I got the spicy chips!

Jack wanted to eat TUM CHIPS. What was the probability for Jack to get the real TUM CHIPS if he just randomly opened 1 bag?

A. 39/80
B. 17/80
C. 39/56
D. 24/56
I think I need to make more bags of chips!
TUM classic
Zzzzz-burp-zzz-burp-zzz
Why do I keep getting spicy chips ?!
TUM

ANSWER

SOLUTION

The number of Jack's real *TUM CHIPS* bags is 80-24-17=39 bags.

As Jack just wants to eat *TUM CHIPS*, he will pick up a bag with the *TUM CHIPS* logo. The total number of bags with *TUM CHIPS* logo is 80-24= 56 bags.

So, the probability for Jack to have the real *TUM CHIPS* is 39/56.

The correct answer is C.

SAILING AROUND the WORLD

Jack, Cool-Doo, Sleepy-Doo and Jr. Z sailed around the world.

They departed in the same year.

I wish I had some chips...

I wish this could be lighter.

Jack and Jr. Z departed on the same **day** of different months.

GET OUT OF MY WAY!

Jack and Cool-Doo departed in the same **month.**

Are we there yet?

Among the 4 boys, who was the last one leaving for his journey?

They departed in the same year.

A

Jr. Z

B

Cool-Doo

D

Jack

C

Sleepy-Doo

ANSWER

SOLUTION

Jack departs on June 15th because he is the only boy who departs in the same day of different months with Jr. Z and departs in the same month with Cool-Doo.

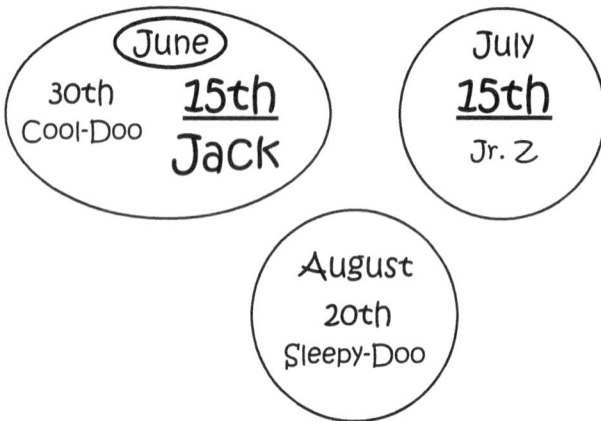

Then the last one is Sleepy-Doo.

The correct answer is C.

THE
MOLE
PATROL

Jr. Z built a square
castle on Z Island.
It's called Z Castle.
Jr. Z commanded a robot
mole to patrol around it.
The mole moved in an even
speed at 1M/second and
it finished one round
in 4 minutes.

Mush,
Mush,
Head up!

Okay moles, listen up. I split the square castle into **2** rectangular zones as shown on this map. One of you two patrolls the right zone, and the other patrolls the left zone. Clear?

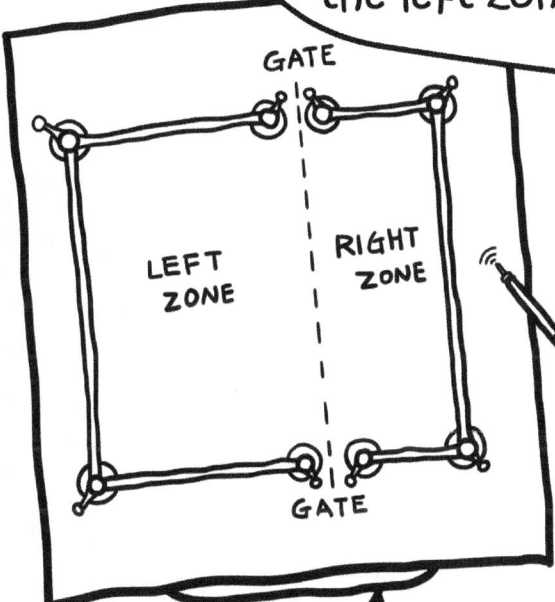

GATE

LEFT ZONE   RIGHT ZONE

GATE

Why do I have to patrol the bigger side?

Be quiet!

I hope it's not my turn yet...

You moles must patrol in a same and even speed at 2M/second !

Yes Sir! According to my calculation, I can use 1 minute and 40 seconds to patrol around the left zone once!

ANSWER

SOLUTION

The perimeter of the square castle is:
1M/sec × 4min × 60 sec/min = 240M

Each side of the square castle is: 240M/4=60M
The perimeter of the left zone is:
2M/sec × (60sec + 40sec) = 200M

X=200M/2-60M=40M
Y=60M-40M=20M

The perimeter of the right zone is:
(20M+60M)x2=160M

The time for the mole patrolling around the right
zone to finish 1 round is:
160M/2M/sec=80sec (1min 20sec)

The correct answer is B.

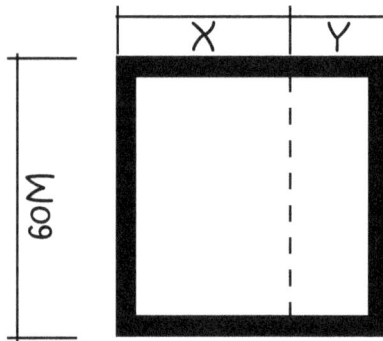

TUM CAR RACING

TUM CAR RACING

The average time of Jack's team is 20 minutes which is ranked as the second place. The first place is 19.5 minutes, and the third place is 20.5 minutes.

Cut it out, Jack!

No, no, NO!

TUM CAR RACING

ERROR

Whoops - I accidently recorded Jack's time wrong. His actual time was **18 minutes**, but it was recorded as **21 minutes**.

Yay!

Just look at what you did!

ANSWER

SOLUTION

The 3 boys' total time should be 21-18=3 minutes less.

After distributing 3 minutes to 3 boys, their average time will be 1 minute less.

So, their actual average time is 20-1=19 minutes.
Their ranking should be the 1st place.

The correct answer is B.

Bicycles and Tricycles

ANSWER

D

SOLUTION

If there are only bicycles, Jack needs only 7×2=14 wheels.

There are 18-14=4 extra wheels.

Why are there 4 extra wheels?

Because tricycles have more wheels than bicycles.

A tricycle has 1 more wheel than a bicycle, so there are 4/1=4 tricycles to make 4 extra wheels, and there are 7-4= 3 bicycles.

The correct answer is D.

Cuts in a Cake

ANSWER

SOLUTION

Since Jack also wants a piece of cake (of course!), there are 12 people altogether.

For 2 cakes, each cake needs to be cut into 6 pieces.

6 pieces need 5 cuts, so altogether there will be 10 cuts.

The correct answer is C.

Who Will Eat the Pizza?

SHAKE
SHAKE

What's the probability for me to eat the pizza by **myself?**

PAPA GREEN'S **PIZZA**

ANSWER

SOLUTION

If Cool-Doo's possibility is based on the sum of smaller than 11, Jack's possibility is based on the sum of greater than or equal to 11.

There are only 3 possibilities for Jack to get a sum of greater than or equal to 11 on 1 throw of 2 fair dice.
5 and 6
6 and 5
6 and 6

The total number of possibilities on tossing 2 fair cubic dice is 6×6=36.

So, the probability for Jack to eat pizza is only 3 out of 36 which is 1/12.

The correct answer is A.

"Jack, your instinct is right, run!"

About the Author

by Andrew, 2007

Andrew Feng

"Myths can be true; fairy tales can be true; even lies can be true. So, why not my dreams?"

Who made up this quote?

Andrew Feng did!

Born on a snowy day, he has always loved drawing doodles from his imagination, whether it's about ordinary Joes traveling around the world or extraordinary guys trying to defeat super villains.

Now, he enjoys drawing comics, reading, writing, swiming, playing the guitar, table tennis, tennis, and basketball, all with his best buddies.

Andrew is not sure what to be when he grows up, but he does know one thing — he will be an awesordinary (awesome + ordinary) guy!

I LovE You Dal

by Adrew , 2007

Peter Feng

Peter is a realtor working in Great Tronto Area. He is neither a writer nor a professional illustrator. English is not even his first language. In 2008, his wife had a miscarriage that made his son Andrew very upset because he always dreamed of having a little brother. To cheer up his son, Peter created an imaginary brother Cool-Doo for Andrew and started creating Cool-Doo stories together with him. With the passion for creating a new family tradition, Peter and his son started learning creative writing from books, the Internet, teachers, writers and editors. With the help and support of family, friends and professional editors, Peter and Andrew published a children's novel, *TUM — The Unmoved Mover,* and a math comic series, *Cool-Doo Math.*

Peter loves the unmeasured, vast expanse of the ocean. He always sees himself as a sailor in the crow's nest looking beyond the horizon, a sailor who never gives up exploring and searching for a new continent.

by Adrew , 2009

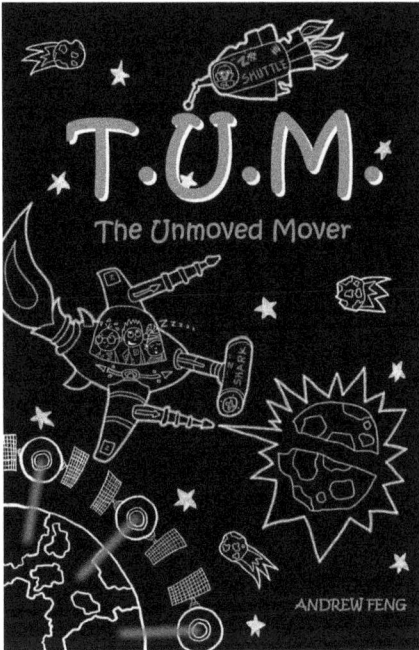

Do you get along with your brother?

Jack doesn't!

Although he has always expected to have a brother to play with, he finds his dream of brotherhood shattered after he gets a really "special" one. This special one always impresses Jack's parents. Plus, this special one also has a special friend of his own, and things always stir up crazily.

Finally, a chance comes for Jack to impress his parents. His hometown is placed in danger while he and the other two special guys are in a space camp, and he only has one night left to become the hero. But, of course, his "special" brother also wants to be the hero.

The clock is ticking...can they make it?

(www.t-u-m.net)

Another Fun Book by Andrew Feng & Peter Feng

Rewriting fables is a very popular practice of creative writing, especially for kids. The process helps children analyze existing fables, think outside of the box to make a new story, and put what they see in their heads onto paper in an ordered, clear, and concise way.

How to Rewrite Fables in a TUM Way uses a comic story to take kids on an exciting and funny journey to learn the process of rewriting fables. Readers will learn the basic structure of a story and how to dressup their writing in a fun way. It also contains examples of rewritten fables.

The characters in the comic story are Jack, Cool-Doo, Sleepy-Doo, and Dr. Green, who are the main characters from the children's novel TUM - The Unmoved Mover. Visit www.t-u-m.net for more information.

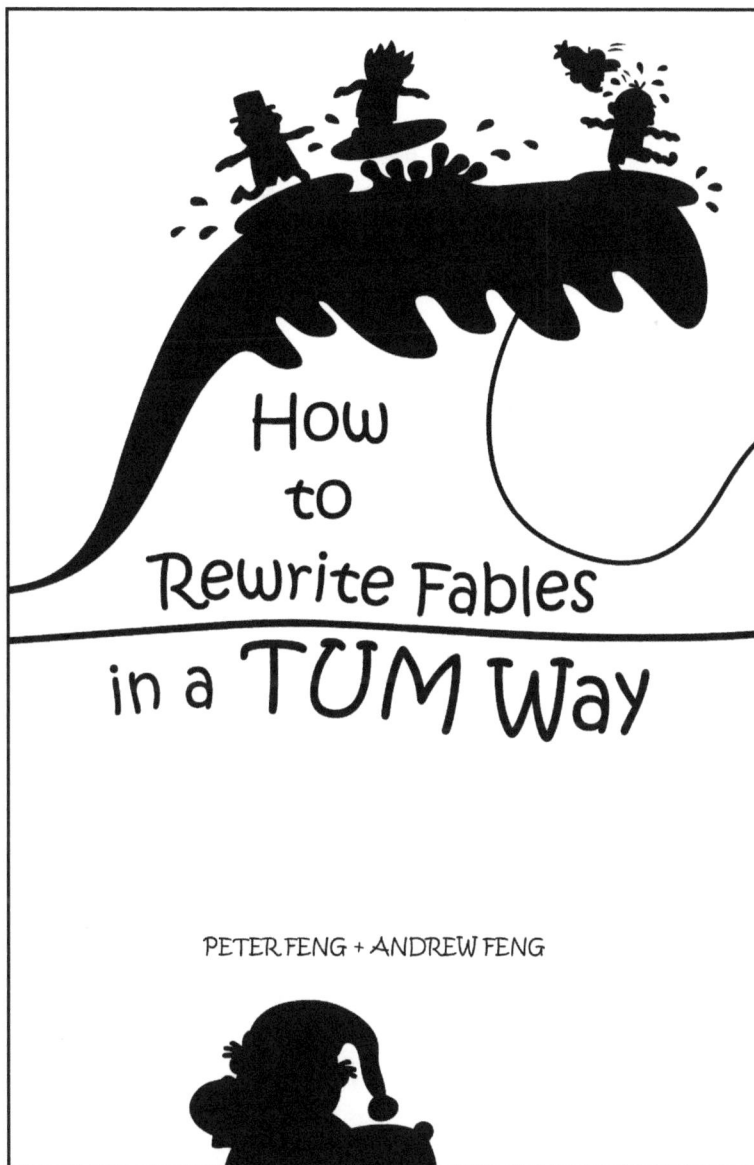

How to Rewrite Fables in a TUM Way

PETER FENG + ANDREW FENG

www.ingramcontent.com/pod-product-compliance
Lightning Source LLC
Chambersburg PA
CBHW061147040426
42445CB00013B/1591